BLAZING A TRAIL

BLAZING A TRAIL

Dorothy Waugh's National Parks Posters

Mark H. Resnick

RIT Press
Rochester, New York

Published and distributed by:
RIT Press
90 Lomb Memorial Drive
Rochester, New York 14623
https://press.rit.edu

Printed in the United States of America

This book was published on the occasion of the exhibition *Blazing a Trail: Dorothy Waugh's National Parks Posters*. The exhibition was organized by the museum Poster House in New York City and was on view there from September 27, 2025, to February 22, 2026. The publisher and author gratefully acknowledge the extraordinary efforts of the museum and its staff with respect to the exhibition and this book.

ISBN 978-1-956313-35-2 (print)
ISBN 978-1-956313-36-9 (electronic)

Library of Congress Cataloging-in-Publication Data

Names: Resnick, Mark H., 1956– author | Poster House host institution
Title: Blazing a trail : Dorothy Waugh's National Parks posters / Mark H. Resnick.
Description: Rochester, New York : RIT Press, [2025]
Identifiers: LCCN 2025027439 (print) | LCCN 2025027440 (ebook) |
ISBN 9781956313352 paperback | ISBN 9781956313369 adobe pdf
Subjects: LCSH: Waugh, Dorothy—Exhibitions | United States. National Park Service—Art patronage—Exhibitions | National parks and reserves—United States—Posters—Exhibitions | Modernism (Art)—United States—Exhibitions
Classification: LCC NC1850.W38 A4 2025 (print) | LCC NC1850.W38 (ebook) |
DDC 744.7/8092—dc23/eng/20250625
LC record available at https://lccn.loc.gov/2025027439
LC ebook record available at https://lccn.loc.gov/2025027440

We gather on the traditional territory of the Onöndowa'ga:' or "the people of the Great Hill." In English, they are known as Seneca people, "the keeper of the western door." They are one of the six nations that make up the sovereign Haudenosaunee Confederacy.

We honor the land on which RIT was built and recognize the unique relationship that the Indigenous stewards have with this land. That relationship is the core of their traditions, cultures, and histories. We recognize the history of genocide, colonization, and assimilation of Indigenous people that took place on this land. Mindful of these histories, we work towards understanding, acknowledging, and ultimately reconciliation.

Cover: *State Parks for Recreation* (detail), Dorothy Waugh. See page 51 for full image.
Designed by Marnie Soom

CONTENTS

"DOROTHY WAUGH IS THE GREATEST TWENTIETH-CENTURY AMERICAN GRAPHIC DESIGNER THAT NO ONE KNOWS ABOUT."

—Christopher Long, architecture and design historian

FOREWORD

Dorothy Waugh's contribution to American design cannot be overstated. Through a serendipitous combination of raw talent, family connections, perseverance, and being in the right place at the right time, she managed to launch herself into a career that no other woman had previously undertaken within the government. Breaking from traditional advertising techniques, she distilled the essence of European modern art through a quintessentially American lens to create vibrant, ambitious, and deeply avant-garde posters promoting the National Park Service during the Great Depression. Moreover, she did it on a budget. Her impact on how the United States saw its public land did not just end there, though; she created the schematics from which previously unskilled workers could interpret architectural plans and build the many park facilities that helped make them attractive destinations. In essence, she is partially responsible for how the United States grew and maintained its love for its national and state parks—a bountiful resource we continue to take advantage of and delight in today.

Blazing a Trail: Dorothy Waugh's National Parks Posters continues a longstanding Poster House tradition of highlighting women's contributions within graphic design history. This publication and its corresponding exhibition are, shockingly, the first to shine a light on Dorothy Waugh's remarkable career—and while the book focuses on her poster designs and their impact on visual culture, another volume could easily delve into any of her other tremendous accomplishments, from book illustration to journalism, fine art to radio and television production. I hope both this text and the show inspire other historians to do that work and expand the Dorothy canon.

Impeccably curated by the American graphic design scholar Mark Resnick, *Blazing a Trail: Dorothy Waugh's National Parks Posters* is the first time every surviving poster by Waugh will be on view in a single exhibition. Drawing primarily from private collections, it reflects the deeply personal connection many poster enthusiasts have for her work—posters that are rarely seen on the market and are coveted by those who desire them. The exhibition also features numerous loans from public institutions, including the National Park Service; the Jones Library in Amherst, Massachusetts; the Vignelli Center for Design Studies; and the Grand Canyon National Park Museum Collection, the stewards of which were generous with both their time and their knowledge. In an era when public service is in an increasingly precarious place, their eagerness to use their resources to contribute to scholarship is commendable and should not be forgotten.

It is also important to note that posters and other ephemera from the WPA period are incredibly scarce. None of this material was meant to survive, and the sheer fact that Mark Resnick and other collaborators on this exhibition were able to mount such an ambitious show proves our collective passion for the medium. Material culture is one of the most accessible and exciting means through which to view history. It is by its nature easy to understand and democratic—characteristics that we strive to adhere to in all of our exhibitions. It is my hope that this publication helps bring to a broader audience knowledge of and appreciation for Dorothy Waugh and the history she helped shape.

Angelina Lippert
Executive Director and Curator
Poster House

PREFACE

Museum exhibitions are small miracles. Everything must come together just right, and shows that feature "rediscovered" artists pose their own additional challenges. The museum takes a greater risk because there isn't a built-in audience, the curator will likely need much more time to ferret out the artist's story, the odds of key works having disappeared will probably increase, and so on. The stakes, too, are different: if the exhibition doesn't materialize, yet another worthy artist, their work remaining out of the public eye, will simply be forgotten.

All of these were considerations in the case of Dorothy Waugh, whose remarkable work for the federal government during the Great Depression put her at the vanguard of American graphic design. Below, I recount some of this exhibition's backstory, along with something else that was outside the show's scope: Waugh was a polymath. Her successful pursuit of many careers likely (and ironically) contributed to her lack of renown today. The exhibition and this accompanying book, among their many aims, finally give Waugh her due.

■ ■ ■

In the 1990s, two of Waugh's national parks posters caught my eye as I passed by the window of a prominent gallery in New York City. Although I was already fairly deep into graphic design history, I knew nothing of Waugh or her work. So, I had to *just look* at the posters without any other point of reference. It was the best kind of introduction, and what I saw was terrific—at once brilliantly executed and accessible, yet leaning toward the avant-garde.

I wanted to know more. For work this good, and especially because the posters were created for a highly visible government campaign, I was confident that I could quickly learn a lot. I was soon disappointed, however, when my research revealed almost nothing or, worse, information that seemed just plain wrong. Nor did I have much time to dig deeper. I had a consuming job as an executive in the film industry, my wife and I were raising our young sons, and, on the side, I was curating a large exhibition and writing an accompanying book on the history of the American poster (both entitled *The American Image: US Posters from the 19th to the 21st Century*).

During the 2010s, however, I was able to tack on a day or two to business and family trips, visiting the many places where I might piece together Waugh's story through primary documents. Armed with my phone's camera, I took countless photos of what I found, for review whenever I might later have the chance. I visited the National Archives; the Waugh Family archives at The Jones Library in Amherst, Massachusetts; the archives of the National Park Service (NPS); the School of the Art Institute of Chicago; and the Library of Congress. I consulted with anyone who might have a good lead. In a parallel nationwide hunt, I managed to find all of Waugh's surviving posters and key related artifacts—the "needles in a haystack" essential for an exhibition—and confirm that their owners would loan them.

Everything was finally starting to come together, and the perfect museum for the exhibition—Poster House in New York City—had expressed interest. But the onset of the COVID-19 pandemic, and my becoming the acting director of the Memphis Brooks Museum of Art in Tennessee, again pushed the exhibition to the side. Finally, during 2024–2025, the exhibition and this book coalesced—a mere three decades after I saw that pair of striking posters in a gallery window!

■ ■ ■

As its title indicates, the exhibition focuses on Waugh's work as a graphic designer for the NPS during the mid-1930s. The show also notes her accomplishments as a landscape architect for the bureau as well as her prior achievements as a multitalented writer-illustrator-designer of her own books. But Waugh would go on to have many other successful careers.

After leaving the NPS in 1937, she founded and led Alfred A. Knopf's Books for Young People in New York City. There, she was responsible for the release of many award-winning books by major writers, often editing, designing, and marketing them herself.

From 1940 to 1965, following her work at Knopf, Waugh was the head of special programs, design, and publicity for the Montclair Public Library in Montclair, New Jersey, which is considered one of the nation's best and most innovative municipal libraries. With the library as home base, Waugh soon also served as the head of public relations for the mayor of Montclair and as a pioneering design educator at top art and design schools; these included Parsons, where she taught the school's first ever course on lettering and typography, and Cooper Union.

She published constantly: more than fifty books (which she wrote, illustrated, designed, and/or edited); journalism for major outlets; poetry; and how-to articles for popular magazines. She was also a cultural commentator and interviewer—in print, on radio (she had her own long-running program), and, occasionally, on television. Throughout, she maintained a fine-art and craft practice. At age ninety-four, she published the last of two deeply researched books on Emily Dickinson—which, insisted the foremost Dickinson scholar, Yale University professor Richard Sewall, "every student of the poet must take into account."

For each of these efforts, Waugh received recognition, and sometimes acclaim, during her life. Yet, when she died in 1996, just shy of age 100, there was no obituary, and little notice has been taken of her since. We can readily speculate on the reasons for this all-too-common scenario: Waugh was a woman; unmarried and without children, she had no surviving immediate family to attend to her legacy; she did her most public work early on, for the NPS; and her artistic practice emphasized design, illustration, and accessible writing, unlikely to be critical darlings.

I'd add something else to this list: Waugh's choice to go as broad in her pursuits as she went deep and to keep moving (for example, she never returned to poster design). Although that approach wasn't bound to bring her the renown of a single, lengthy practice, it reflected her abilities, her curiosity, and a pragmatic need to pay the bills. It reflected who she was.

■ ■ ■

I'd like to thank all of those at Poster House who made the exhibition possible, especially Angelina Lippert (the museum's superb executive director), Ola Baldych (director of design and exhibits), and Melanie Papathomas (registrar). Among the several generous lenders to the exhibition, I must single out the remarkable Jones Library in Amherst, Massachusetts; its Special Collections team, headed by Katherine Whitcomb, has been a resource to me for many years now. I also gratefully acknowledge the careful review of the exhibition text by Nancy Russell, National Park Service History Collection, and Dr. Mary Okin, Living New Deal. This book also gave me the privilege of working once more with the consummate professionals at RIT Press: Laura DiPonzio Heise (director), Marnie Soom (design and marketing specialist), and Alexandra Hoff (managing editor). I owe thanks, as well, to Annaliese Bischoff, Professor Emerita at the University of Massachusetts Amherst; she has generously shared much information about the Waugh family and has become a friend. As ever, I'm grateful for the expert logistical help Amber Blaise provided in Los Angeles. Finally, I thank my wonderful family, who not only indulge but support my quests.

"THERE IS NOTHING SO AMERICAN AS OUR NATIONAL PARKS. THE FUNDAMENTAL IDEA . . . IS THAT THE COUNTRY BELONGS TO THE PEOPLE . . . FOR THE ENRICHMENT OF THE LIVES OF ALL OF US."

—President Franklin D. Roosevelt

A GROUNDBREAKING CAMPAIGN

The seventeen travel posters Dorothy Waugh created for the National Park Service (NPS) between 1934 and 1936 comprise a striking visual record in the history of the Great Depression and mark a turning point in American graphic design. Until now, however, there has been little research on them or on their creator. This exhibition, based on private and government documents, is the first dedicated to Waugh and the first to show all of the campaign's surviving posters.

From the 1870s, America's railroad companies played a critical role in promoting the national parks as tourist destinations—in order, primarily, to increase passenger numbers. Even after the founding of the NPS under President Woodrow Wilson in 1916, the railroads continued to be the main source of such advertising; they issued a steady stream of attractive, if conventional, posters popularizing the parks and the beautiful landscapes on the routes to them. During the Depression, however, the parks took on new importance. President Franklin D. Roosevelt invested heavily in parks tourism, convinced that it would be crucial in restoring the nation's shattered morale and economy.

Although Waugh began her work for the NPS in 1933 as a landscape architect, she was also a highly trained artist. She soon advocated that the bureau produce its own poster campaign, separate from those of the railroads and with its own style and messaging. In 1934, the Roosevelt administration launched National Parks Year, a public-relations initiative that included money for the campaign, whose design was entrusted to Waugh. It was the first time the government had assigned such an ambitious project to a solo designer, let alone a female modernist. Waugh also received the backing of her male supervisor, a senior official within the NPS, who was well aware of her artistic talent. The resulting series of posters, at once avant-garde and accessible, put Waugh at the forefront of what would become the government's expansive presence in American visual culture.

NORTHERN PACIFIC
YELLOWSTONE
PARK
NORTHERN PACIFIC

NORTHERN PACIFIC
North Coast Limited
in the Montana Rockies

Yellowstone Park, 1924

D'après Thomas Moran (1837–1926)

Poster House Permanent Collection

North Coast Limited/Montana Rockies, 1929

Gustav W. Krollman (1888–1962)

Poster House Permanent Collection

- These Northern Pacific Railway posters from the 1920s follow the typical formula of much railroad advertising of the period: Incorporating a third party's dramatic painting, they each depict a specific park, the route to it, or the train itself. A logo identifies the railroad, and minimal text indicates the destination.
- The poster for Yellowstone reproduces the central portion of Thomas Moran's famous oil painting *The Grand Canyon of the Yellowstone*, completed between 1893 and 1901 and now in the collection of the Smithsonian American Art Museum in Washington, DC. A Hudson River School painter, Moran was celebrated for his depictions of the American West. In 1871, he joined the Hayden Geological Survey on its expedition to the area that would become Yellowstone National Park. Moran worked closely with survey photographer William Henry Jackson, making sketches and watercolors that he would use as the basis for his first version of a painting by this name. Along with Jackson's photographs, that enormous work hung in Congress and played a pivotal role in convincing legislators to designate, in 1872, Yellowstone as the first national park.
- The poster for the Montana Rockies reproduces a painting by Gustav Krollman commissioned directly by the railroad company. It depicts the mighty locomotive required to navigate the Bozeman Pass near Yellowstone. As passenger numbers declined in the 1930s, due in part to the rise of automobile travel, the railroad companies emphasized both the power and the comfort of trains.

National Parks/The Adventures of Today Are the Memories of Tomorrow, 1934

Dorothy Waugh (1896–1996)

Private Collection

- Waugh's National Parks poster contrasts starkly with the typical railroad posters of the period. Although it, too, features a dramatic landscape, the composition is solely her own and, largely abstract, does not depict an identifiable location. The text presents a rather poetic message and, of course, there is no corporate logo. The choice of yellow for the water and sky, along with the framing device of staggered black bars, leans toward the avant-garde.
- Waugh's image is an unexpected complement to the text: here, the "adventure" is in the contemplative and silent act of fishing in a mountain lake.
- This poster also evokes the harmonious coexistence of humans and nature that has been a core principle and practice of Indigenous people in the Americas for millennia. Such harmony was also espoused by nineteenth-century American naturalists, philosophers, and social reformers like Henry David Thoreau, who cautioned that modern society alienates us from nature's physical and spiritual sustenance.

the ADVENTURES of TODAY are the
MEMORIES of TOMORROW
NATIONAL
PARKS
DOROTHY WAUGH

"MY FATHER SENT ME TO THE SCHOOL OF THE ART INSTITUTE OF CHICAGO TO MAKE ME MORE INDEPENDENT. IT WORKED TOO WELL!"

—Dorothy Waugh

PREPARATION

Dorothy Waugh was first exposed to landscape architecture as a youngster. Her father, Frank Waugh, had founded one of the nation's earliest landscape architecture programs (at the Massachusetts Agricultural College, now the University of Massachusetts Amherst), and she frequently sat in on his classes. Her focus on the landscape would inform much of her later work, especially her National Park Service posters.

In 1916, Waugh enrolled at the School of the Art Institute of Chicago (SAIC), but her studies were disrupted after only a year by the entry of the United States into World War I. Over the next ten years, she would continue to study in her father's program, work as a landscape architect in a number of states, and take art classes at night. Waugh reenrolled at SAIC in 1926 at the age of thirty. There, she was exposed to European avant-garde art and design movements gaining traction in the United States. She began to develop her own distinctive brand of American modernism, in which she freely combined elements from those movements while embracing commercial illustration and incorporating American subject matter and iconography.

After graduating in 1928, Waugh worked as an illustrator, copywriter, and designer for various publishing and advertising firms in Chicago. In 1931, Henry Holt and Co. published *Among the Leaves and Grasses*, Waugh's book for young adults; her modernist illustrations and lettering in it anticipate the visual language of her National Park Service posters. Despite the Depression, the book's success encouraged her to move to New York City to pursue a career in publishing.

Anthony Hansen
NEW ENGLAND
AMERICA'S HISTORIC SUMMERLAND
NEW YORK CENTRAL LINES

New England/New York Central Lines, c. 1930

Anthony Hansen (Dates Unknown)

Courtesy of David and Lucinda Pollack

- A composite of New England scenery, this poster captures the pastoral region that inspired Waugh's lifelong study of nature. It also reflects the illustrational style that prevailed in American travel posters through much of the 1930s.
- Late in her life, Waugh wrote of Amherst, "This wonderful environment became the playground of six Waugh children," who also happily assisted "in the college's model orchards, vineyards, prize herds, arboretums, and sheepcotes."
- Commercial artist Anthony Hansen's picturesque design champions travel to "America's Historic Summerland." He presents the landscape in realistic depth, color, and detail without the abstraction that Waugh employed in her posters for the National Park Service. His serif lettering, reminiscent of typefaces popular in the eighteenth and nineteenth centuries, accords with the poster's promotion of the relatively unchanged countryside as a retreat from modernity.

Frank Waugh, c. 1925
Photographer Unknown
Collection of Annaliese Bischoff, ASLA, Professor Emerita

Dorothy and Sidney Waugh, c. 1915
Photographer Unknown
Courtesy of The Jones Library, Inc., Amherst, Massachusetts

- Frank Waugh, like his daughter Dorothy, was a polymath. He was an accomplished printmaker, photographer, and musician whose interdisciplinary approach to teaching landscape architecture was evident in frequent field trips with his young children, who went on to have illustrious careers. He assigned them projects based on their observation of nature, including specimen drawings, poems, essays, and musical performances.
- Dorothy is photographed painting from nature during her high school years, observed by her younger brother, Sidney (who would later become a renowned sculptor and the head of design at Steuben Glass Works). After graduating, Dorothy moved to Boston for a year, where she studied at the Massachusetts College of Art and worked at a landscape architecture firm before enrolling in the School of the Art Institute of Chicago (SAIC).

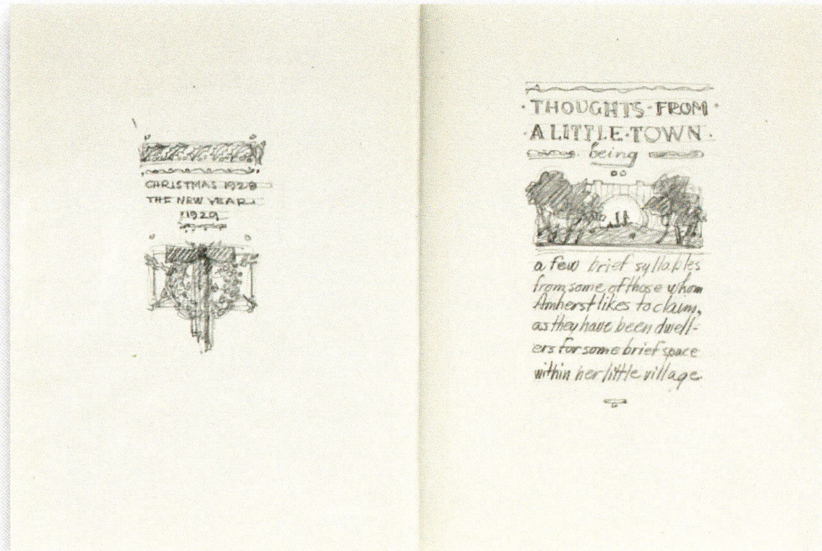

Thoughts from a Little Town, 1928

Dorothy Waugh (1896–1996)

Courtesy of The Jones Library, Inc., Amherst, Massachusetts

- Waugh created this booklet while in art school at SAIC. She presented it to the Jones Library in Amherst, Massachusetts, as a rough study, hoping for a commission (unrealized) to produce it as a promotional item for the library and town during the Christmas season. It features illustrated poems by local luminaries, including Robert Frost and Emily Dickinson—the latter a lifelong subject of Waugh's own art and writing.
- The booklet's design is heavily influenced by the Arts and Crafts movement, an artistic response to industrialization that flourished in the United States roughly between 1900 and 1920. Celebrating the artist-maker, the movement emphasized traditional craft skills and making by hand; motifs and materials derived from nature; and simplicity of design and quality in construction, with ornament as a complement to function.
- Nineteenth-century education reform had opened the door for women to attend art schools. They became central to the Arts and Crafts movement as professional artists, designers, teachers, authors, and entrepreneurs across all of the fine and applied arts.
- *Thoughts from a Little Town* reflects the movement's decrial of the uniformity of machine-made books and bindings. Entirely handmade by Waugh, the booklet's cover epitomizes the Arts and Crafts aesthetic, and its contents feature her pencil lettering and drawings.

Among the Leaves and Grasses, 1931

Dorothy Waugh (1896–1996)

Left: *Courtesy of The Jones Library, Inc., Amherst, Massachusetts*

Right: *Private Collection*

- This children's book likely started as one of Waugh's projects at SAIC. She created the sketches for its striking Art Deco illustrations and lettering in watercolor, just as she did later for the National Park Service posters. Waugh's mastery of this medium allowed her to render areas of flat color usually associated with modernist woodblock or silkscreen printing.
- The book was aimed at young readers curious about insects, highlighting seven of the most common species in vibrant detail. Vetted by an entomologist, it also reflected Waugh's own aptitude for science and was the first of many publications that showcased her talent for accessible scholarship.
- The book became a calling card as Waugh embarked on a publishing career that would see her write, illustrate, design, and edit some fifty books and numerous periodicals. Several of her books won the American Institute of Graphic Arts' contest, held annually from 1941 on, for the fifty best-designed books of the year.
- In the late nineteenth and early twentieth centuries, female artists were generally excluded from art classes featuring human models; accordingly, they often focused on natural subjects, especially plants, insects, and animals. For many of them, the illustration of books on nature, travelogues, and periodicals became a regular source of income.

among the leaves and grasses
by dorothy waugh
henry holt + company

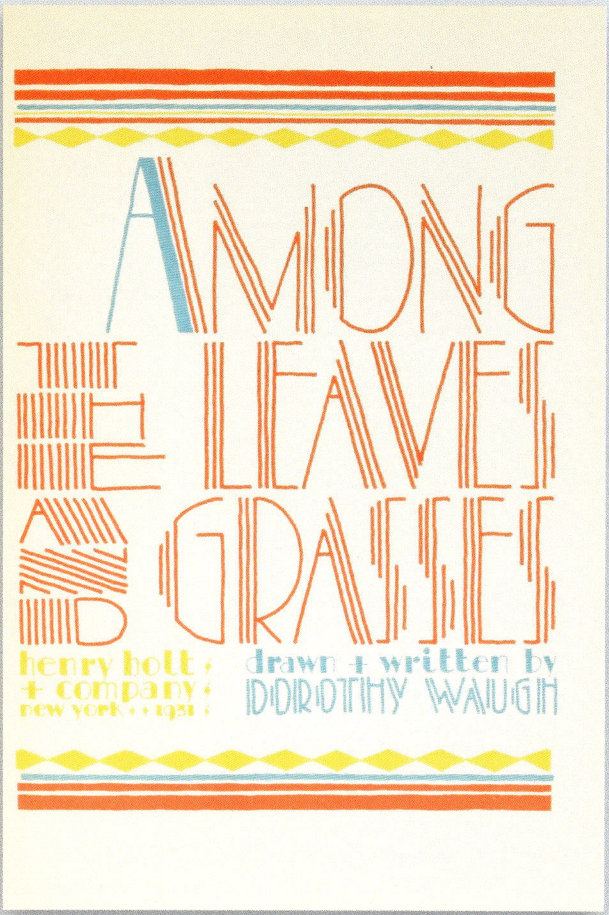
AMONG THE LEAVES AND GRASSES
henry holt + company new york 1931
drawn + written by
DOROTHY WAUGH

"WE DIDN'T HAVE FOOD. WE DIDN'T HAVE JOBS. I DON'T THINK PEOPLE REALIZE HOW CLOSE THIS NATION CAME TO HAVING A REVOLUTION."

—Vincente Ximenes, Civilian Conservation Corps worker

A NEW DEAL AND THE CIVILIAN CONSERVATION CORPS

When Franklin D. Roosevelt became president of the United States in March 1933, the country was in the depths of the Depression. His response was a New Deal for Americans that included the introduction of regulatory agencies, social service programs, and public works projects. His most successful and popular jobs program was the Civilian Conservation Corps (CCC), established in his first month in office with a mandate to address the country's economic and environmental crises. It was the fastest peacetime mobilization of personnel and the largest conservation effort in US history, ultimately putting three million unemployed young men to work in parks, plains, and forests.

A staunch conservationist, Roosevelt believed that stewardship of the country's magnificent, yet neglected, public lands would also dramatically increase tourism—stimulating the economy, both nationally and locally, and restoring Americans' decimated pride and well-being. Although most Americans could not afford to travel abroad, they might be enticed to travel domestically, spending what they could and thus contributing to the country's economic recovery.

A broad range of basic structures—cabins, campgrounds, administrative facilities, and more—were soon required to accommodate the increasing number of visitors to national and state parks. Conrad Wirth, an assistant director of the NPS, oversaw the massive project in the state parks through the CCC. The young men hired to build the new park infrastructure, however, were inexperienced, were mostly unable to read blueprints or complicated text, and had no instruction manual to guide them. To address the problem, in August 1933, Wirth hired Waugh as a landscape architect. She was to gather blueprints of exemplary buildings from around the country, translate them into easily understood, accurate illustrational drawings supplemented by basic construction guidelines, and oversee their publication in the *Portfolio of Park Structures and Facilities*. Rushed to the field in loose-leaf installments, the straightforward yet artistic *Portfolio* was considered a major success, keeping the young men working while ensuring the building program's nationwide consistency and quality. Her work on the project also provided Waugh with a deeper understanding of the National Park Service, which would prove indispensable as she tackled the subsequent poster campaign. By 1934, Waugh, one of only two women in prominent positions within the NPS, had become the key figure in the bureau's production of materials requiring sophisticated graphic design.

A YOUNG MAN'S OPPORTUNITY
CCC
FOR WORK PLAY STUDY & HEALTH
UNITED STATES
CCC
CIVILIAN CONSERVATION CORPS
Bender
APPLICATIONS TAKEN BY
ILLINOIS EMERGENCY RELIEF COMMISSION
ILLINOIS SELECTING AGENCY
MADE BY ILLINOIS WPA-ART PROJECT CHICAGO

CCC/A Young Man's Opportunity, 1941

Albert M. Bender (Dates Unknown)

Private Collection

- The CCC employed young men between the ages of eighteen and twenty-five to conserve and develop public land through manual labor. Participants usually arrived at a given site with little work experience. Only 11 percent of them had received a high school education, and up to 70 percent were malnourished and poorly clothed, reflecting the poverty caused by the Depression and the Dust Bowl. The latter was an ecological disaster in the Great Plains states caused by unprecedented drought and erosion that wasmade worse due to generations of prior mismanagement; it decimated livestock, crops, and wildlife while displacing millions of people.
- In addition to providing the men with employment, the CCC improved their health, morale, and education and enabled them to develop specialized and marketable vocational skills. Approximately 85 percent of their monthly salary of $30 ($728 today) was sent home to support their families. The economy of each community in which a CCC camp was located also benefited, due to government procurements and the workers' incidental spending. The program operated until 1942, when the United States entered World War II and the young men were needed by the military.
- This poster was created by Albert Bender, a designer in the Federal Art Project (FAP), several years after Waugh's NPS designs. The FAP, created under the auspices of the Works Progress Administration, was a New Deal initiative that provided work for unemployed artists of all types and skill levels. It included poster divisions located in various regions of the country that served the promotional needs of an exhaustive list of federal, state, and local government clients, as well as some in the private sector.

Conrad Wirth, 1934
Photographer Unknown
Courtesy of National Park Service, National Park Service History Collection, HFCA 3089

Dorothy Waugh, c. 1930
Photographer Unknown
Courtesy of The Jones Library, Inc., Amherst, Massachusetts

- Conrad Wirth first met Waugh around 1917 when he was studying under her father at Massachusetts Agricultural College (now the University of Massachusetts Amherst). Wirth recognized Waugh's talent and employed her from 1926 to 1927 as a landscape architect at his firm.
- NPS records indicate that their working relationship was characterized above all by mutual respect and an insistence on quality. From Wirth's position of growing authority—he would ultimately head the NPS—he invariably acknowledged Waugh's ability, strongly supported her creative efforts, and furthered her advancement, in both title and salary, within the bureau.
- Waugh brought a unique set of skills to the NPS and was quite confident in them, once stating that "I know of no other illustrator who has my landscape architecture experience . . . and no other landscape architect who has my experience with illustration, type arrangement, and writing."

"A chief objection was that it would be difficult for a woman. In actual practice I have found that seldom proves to be a real objection when a case is put to the test."

—Dorothy Waugh

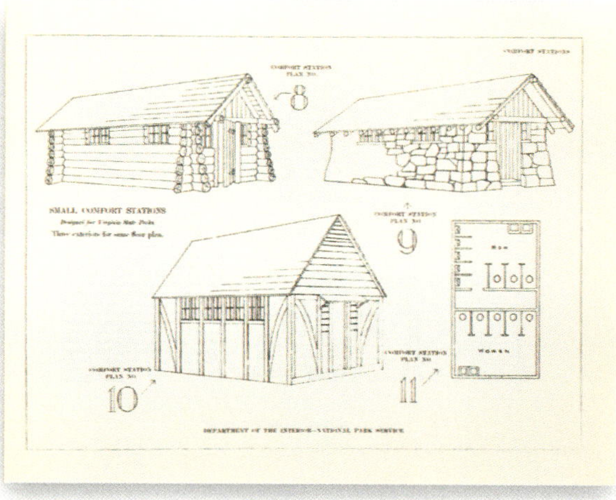

Portfolio of Park Structures and Facilities, 1933–34

Dorothy Waugh (1896–1996)

Courtesy of National Park Service, National Park Service History Collection, HFCA 2995

Diagram for Small Comfort Station, 1933

Dorothy Waugh (1896–1996)

Courtesy of National Park Service, National Park Service History Collection, HFCA 2999

- The *Portfolio* structures were built by the CCC in the "rustic style," which featured local stone and timber to complement the surrounding landscape. Among other visitor amenities, these buildings included cabins, sanitary facilities, picnic and camping grounds, lodges, amphitheaters, museums, and administrative quarters—many of which survive today.
- Here, Waugh presents her plans for a "small comfort station" (a restroom with flush toilets) to guide the CCC's construction. These facilities made travel to national and state parks more appealing and increasingly incorporated modern, electricity-driven plumbing still lacking in much of the country.
- Although Waugh initially worked alone on the drawings for the *Portfolio*, the size and urgency of the project meant that she was eventually authorized to hire and supervise a team of male draftsmen to help her complete it. In the field, the drawings could be supplemented as necessary by professional architects hired by the government to oversee construction.

> "IN NO SMALL MEASURE, ARTISTS SAVED [THE NATIONAL PARKS] BY MAKING THEM UNFORGETTABLE. THE PARKS THEMSELVES WERE NEVER ENOUGH."
>
> —Alfred Runte, environmental historian

IF YOU PROMOTE IT, THEY WILL COME

To spur tourism, the new stewardship and development of the parks would have to be aggressively promoted. Waugh, who knew the power of the medium, advocated for a poster campaign. Wirth, however, was hamstrung: Not only had the National Park Service never issued its own posters, but it lacked the money to do so. An opening finally came when the Roosevelt administration designated 1934 "National Parks Year" and allocated a small sum for a marketing campaign. Between 1934 and 1936, Waugh delivered the now-funded poster designs in batches. For each design, she created a watercolor composition on a paper board that was the same size as the final poster, then oversaw its translation into a lithographic print. With no money for extra materials, she had to get both the idea and its execution exactly right on the first attempt.

Wirth allowed Waugh a great deal of creative freedom. Her posters for the NPS would have looked quite new and modern to the public, especially in comparison to those issued by the railroad companies. Her style covered a very broad range, from illustrational in the manner of children's books to cutting-edge modernist, and each design incorporated its own, often innovative lettering. Waugh's posters also conveyed new messages, focusing variously on the regenerative spirit of the parks (and, by extension, of the New Deal); the national park system as a unified whole; the burgeoning state parks; the parks as places for year-round, affordable recreation; and the parks and national monuments as repositories of the country's history.

Thousands of copies of Waugh's posters were printed and distributed throughout the United States (and a few internationally). Displayed in bus and railroad stations, travel agencies, post offices, and other public places, they contributed to a two-and-a-half fold increase in the number of visitors to the national parks by 1937.

The Lure of the National Parks, 1934

Dorothy Waugh (1896–1966)

Private Collection

- By 1933, there were many more national parks than there were at the NPS's founding in 1916, and the additional parks, per the bureau's plan, were frequently located in states that used to have none.
- Amid this strategic growth, Waugh's first ten posters (referred to by the NPS as the "Spring" and "Winter" series) were broadly institutional designs that did not reference any particular park. They typify Waugh's artistic approach: modernist yet accessible, never entirely abandoning the American taste for realistic depiction.
- This Spring series poster alludes to the magnetic pull of the parks and the great outdoors. Its horizontal, tightly cropped image of men on horseback suggests a sequence from a quintessentially American film genre, the Western. Moviegoing was enormously popular during the Depression, peaking in 1936 at a weekly audience of eighty-eight million. Here, Waugh borrows from the appeal of the movies to promote the park system.
- Waugh used slogan-like captions or titles, like the one seen here, only in the Spring series. Although the NPS publicity department provided her with the texts, she heavily edited them to make them shorter and catchier.

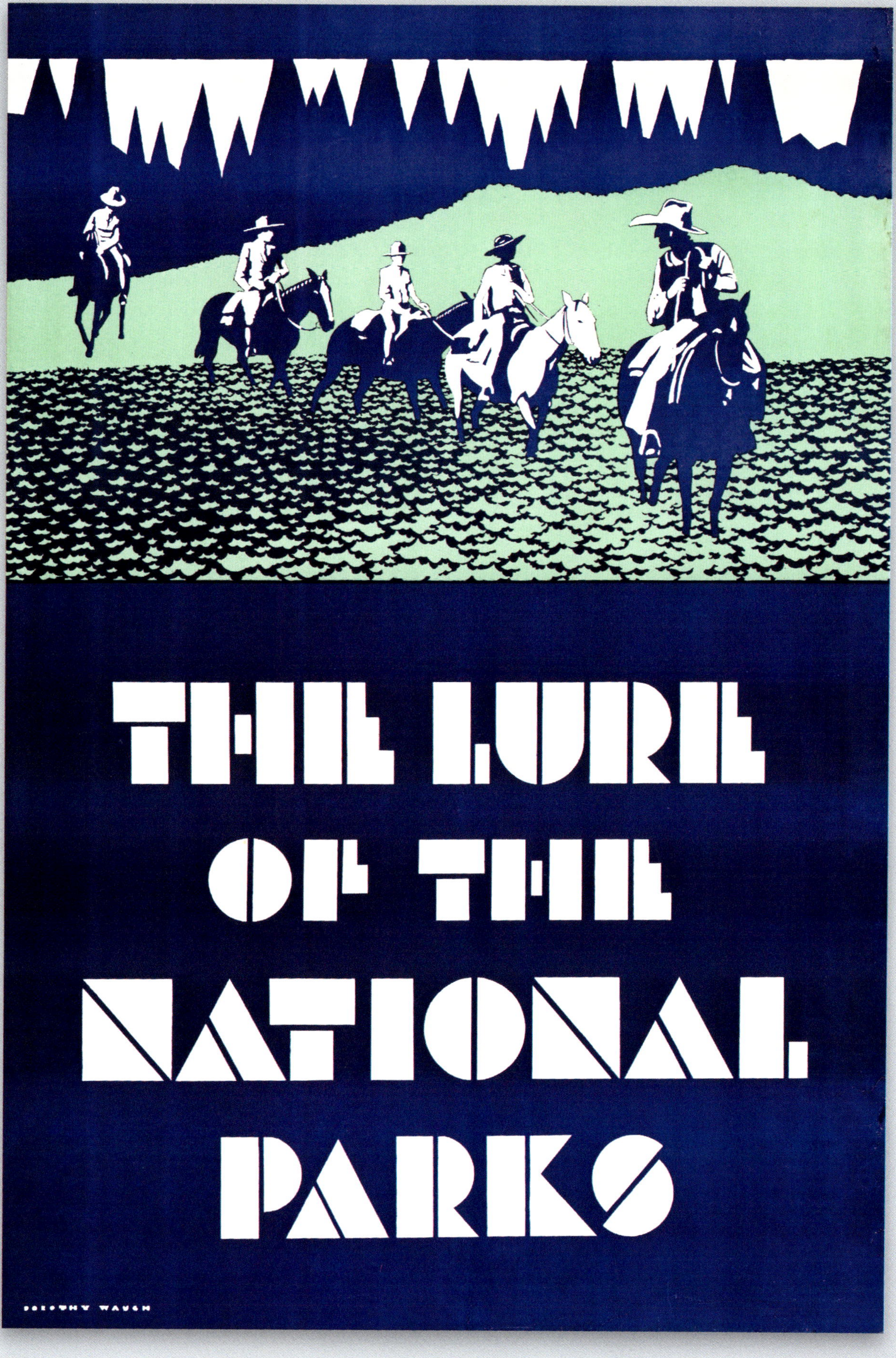
THE LURE
OF THE
NATIONAL
PARKS
DOROTHY WAUGH

where the deer and
the antelope play
DOROTHY WAUGH
National Parks

National Parks/Where the Deer and the Antelope Play, 1934

Dorothy Waugh (1896–1996)

Private Collection

- The campaign highlighted three key aspects of parks tourism: engagement with nature, recreation, and culture. Here, nature is ascendant as a deer roams undisturbed in a pristine landscape. The subtext is that the preservation of nature is compatible with parks tourism.
- The title of this poster comes from Roosevelt's favorite song, "Home on the Range," which the popular singer Bing Crosby had made a hit just as Waugh started working at the NPS. A traditional ballad of the American West, the song was based on a poem written in the early 1870s by Kansas homesteader Dr. Brewster M. Higley and was gradually spread to other ranching states by cowboys working the cattle trade.
- Due to extreme budget constraints, Waugh often used only one or two colors in her posters, a design challenge that further sparked her creativity. Here, yellow rays of the sun backlight the scene, creating striking brown silhouettes of natural forms. Waugh's homespun cursive lettering, which is in keeping with the song's folk quality, incorporates the white of the paper as a third color.

National Parks/Mystery Veils the Desert, 1934

Dorothy Waugh (1896–1996)

Private Collection

- With the establishment of Death Valley as a national monument in 1933 and Joshua Tree in 1936, the NPS added two major sites to its desert portfolio (they would both be designated national parks in 1994).
- Even with the CCC's development efforts, many Americans hesitated to visit these remote locations, worried about the harsh desert climate and unfamiliar wildlife. Waugh's poster contributed to efforts to reassure them, emphasizing special and enduring qualities of the desert: the exceptional clarity of its night sky and the solitude and mystery to be found in its otherworldly landscape.
- Standing in for the entire Southwest, this desert scene presents a quiet drama in which a lone horseman (who may be a park ranger) is dwarfed by the seemingly infinite cosmos. Waugh's simple, almost pictographic handling of the image recalls her talent as a children's book illustrator.

MYSTERY VEILS THE DESERT
National Parks
DOROTHY WAUGH

DOROTHY WAUGH
his hunting ground
of yesterday
NATIONAL PARKS

National Parks/His Hunting Ground of Yesterday, 1934

Dorothy Waugh (1896–1996)

Private Collection

Blackfeet Indians at Glacier National Park, c. 1916

Ernest L. Crandall (1870–1950)

Courtesy of National Park Service, National Park Service History Collection

- The government's establishment of many of the national parks resulted in the forced removal of Native Americans from their ancestral lands, destruction of their ways of life, and misrepresentation of their diverse cultures. This poster, although beautiful, relies on the spectacle of a "vanishing race" to promote tourism—in effect romanticizing such displacement and cultural erasure.
- Indigenous people were typically portrayed by others via stereotypes that reduced them to "noble savages," brutal warlords, and cigar-and-trinket sellers, without tribal identifiers or individual characteristics. Waugh's depiction is relatively dignified, but it does employ some reductive tropes: in lieu of showing any individual's face, the focus is on a generic feathered headdress, bow, and clothing.
- This is the only time Waugh based an NPS poster directly on an existing image: a staged photograph of Blackfeet Indians at Glacier National Park, Montana, published in *The National Parks Portfolio* of 1931. She chose, however, to replace the staff of the figure in the photograph with a bow, thus reinforcing the conception of Native Americans as hunters—once a reality but by then a hollow stereotype.

New Mexico and Arizona Rockies, 1932

Kenneth Willmarth (1889–1975) and William Willmarth (1898–1984)

Poster House Permanent Collection

- In 1932, with passenger numbers declining due to the economic downturn and competition from the automobile, a collective of railroad companies held a contest aimed at updating their poster designs.
- The winning posters made stylistic advances, deploying somewhat more abstract forms and a greater variety of lettering than their predecessors. Although this poster reflects those changes, it is still less modernist than Waugh's designs from around the same time, particularly in its reliance on detailed illustration to advance the narrative.
- Posters that featured Native Americans continued to incorporate stereotypes that would persist in advertising for decades. This scene highlights the gross power imbalance between a well-heeled tourist and a Native American craftsman. The woman, towering over the submissive Indigenous figure, appears to haggle with him over a strand of beads. This implied dominance accorded with the prevailing notion that white people were the best stewards of the land and its resources.

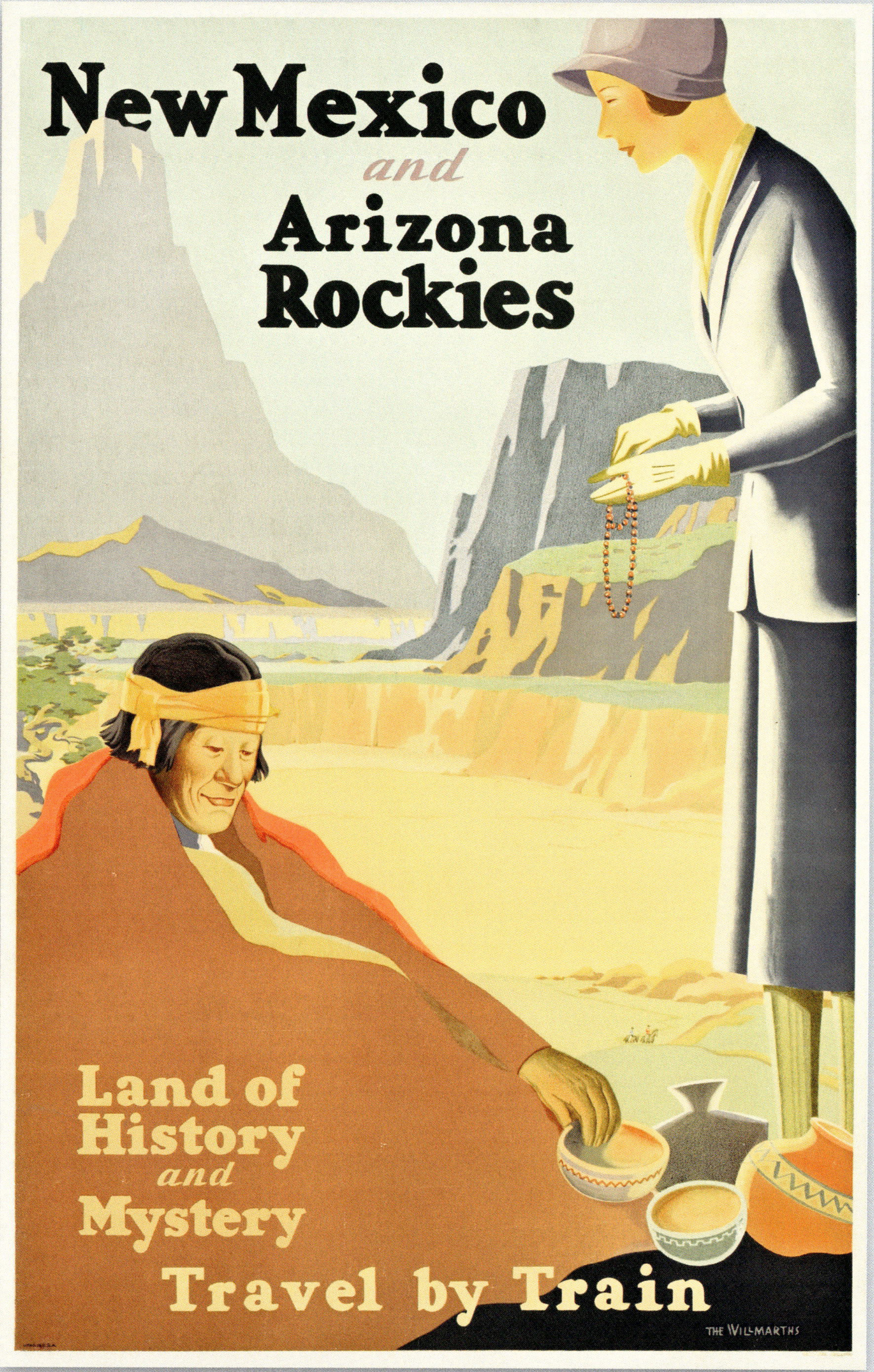
New Mexico
and
Arizona
Rockies
Land of
History
and
Mystery
Travel by Train
THE WILLMARTHS

Life at its best
National Parks

National Parks/Life at Its Best, 1934

Dorothy Waugh (1896–1996)

Private Collection

- Waugh's image of wilderness, fellowship, and living off the land promotes the national parks as a tonic for the stifling constraints of the Depression and of urban life in general. Its successful design relies on a complex visual rhythm in which each set of forms, rising and falling, echoes another: The long slopes of the mountain peaks, the staccato arrangement of the tree line, and the trio of cowboys around a comforting fire. Even the lettering of the words "National Parks" evokes the contours of a mountain range.
- Waugh's depiction may well have been influenced by the "campfire origin story" of the first national park. On September 19, 1870, the story relates, three explorers gathered around a campfire near the junction of two rivers in the Yellowstone area. One of them, Cornelius Hedges, came up with the idea, quickly embraced by the other two men, of setting aside Yellowstone's geyser basins and adjacent lands as a national park. Although many historians have challenged the accuracy of this creation story, its symbolic power persists.
- Amid the Depression, the tagline "life at its best" may seem absurdly optimistic. It nonetheless reflects the prevailing sentiment of the campaign: America remains a land of abundant beauty and natural resources, and the national parks system offers everyone access to these riches.

Years of Dust, 1937

Ben Shahn (1898–1969)

Private Collection

- The sunniness of Waugh's posters offered viewers a respite from much of the imagery produced during the Depression. Ben Shahn's *Years of Dust* is a prime example of Social Realism, an art movement that exposed the period's social ills in frank, often gritty depictions of the struggles of ordinary people.
- Shahn, who had been hired in 1935 as a documentary photographer for the federal government, based this design on one of his photographs that captured the human toll of the Dust Bowl.

YEARS OF DUST
DUST STORM
RESETTLEMENT ADMINISTRATION
Rescues Victims
Restores Land to Proper Use

NATIONAL PARKS
WINTER SPORTS

National Parks/Winter Sports, 1935

Dorothy Waugh (1896–1996)

Private Collection

- For the greatest economic impact, parks tourism had to be enticing year-round; thus, the colder months, when travel was less popular, became a particular focus of the bureau.
- In her Winter series, Waugh dispensed with majestic scenery and wildlife in favor of stylized figures reveling in a panoply of winter sports.
- This complex, carefully balanced Art Deco montage is a good example of Waugh's design sophistication. She plays with cropping, detail, and scale: the snowflakes, even when shown only in part, are highly individualized and as large as the figures, whose faces remain featureless. Waugh further defies convention by substituting a flat black background for snow and ice, enhancing the visual impact and three-dimensionality of the poster's more colorful elements. The text reinforces the illusion of depth, as the phrase "winter sports" appears to project while "national parks" recedes.
- Featuring seven colors, the poster also reflects Waugh's canny management of a small, fixed budget. By employing a limited, cost-saving palette in most of her designs, she could be more lavish with color in a few posters like this one.

National Parks/Skiing, 1935

Dorothy Waugh (1896–1996)

Collection of Cathy M. Kaplan

- Skiing soon became an attraction in select national parks, with the CCC helping to create ski trails. The young men cut them in various parts of the country—from New Hampshire, where they were brought in to finish the first trail ever attempted on a 4,000-foot mountain, to national parks in the western states. In the 1930s, some national parks also hosted high-stakes ski competitions.
- Although skiing was appealing to many tourists, conservationists objected to its impact on the land, due first to the ski trails and then to the ski lifts and other structures. Their complaints reflected a longstanding divide between those favoring the public use of parks and those dedicated to preservation—a tension that continues today as the parks balance economic concerns with fears about the effects of overtourism.
- Here, Waugh promotes the exciting new opportunities for downhill skiing offered by the parks. She depicts a lone woman speeding fearlessly down a slope comprised of blue and white stripes that combine with red accents in a subtle nod to the federal government's role in the project.

dorothy
waugh
national
parks
skiing

WINTER SPORTS
NATIONAL & STATE PARKS

National and State Parks/Winter Sports, 1936

Dorothy Waugh (1896–1996)

Private Collection

- For those not interested in downhill skiing, this poster points to the advantages of trekking on flat ground: a couple can spend extended time together at a slower pace in a beautiful setting, interrupted only by gently falling snow.
- Waugh's poster epitomizes Art Deco romance, from the elegant, fused forms of the stylish couple—a sculptural "snow man" and "snow woman" against a flat, teal background—to the stylized lettering in banners that again create a sense of depth.

SKIING
SKATING
NATIONAL and
STATE PARKS
SLIDING
SLEIGHING
U.S. GOVERNMENT PRINTING OFFICE
DOROTHY WAUGH

National and State Parks, 1936

Dorothy Waugh (1896–1996)

Collection of Cathy M. Kaplan

Keen's, c. 1940

Sascha Maurer (1897–1961)

Poster House Permanent Collection

- Waugh's poster, at left, is unlike any previously created by an American designer. It fuses elements associated with the European avant-garde, such as geometric forms, flat primary colors, and sans-serif lettering, with Waugh's own unique visual language.
- With its reduction of the robot-like skier to bold geometries, the poster has a futuristic quality not found elsewhere in Waugh's body of work. The black banners of text in front of the skier cleverly double as a ski-racing gate, suggesting the action to come.
- The audacity of Waugh's design is perhaps best understood in comparison to Sascha Maurer's take on the same subject. A well-known European modernist, Maurer is often credited as one of the artists who brought avant-garde poster design to the United States. Here, however, he avoids aesthetic risk, sticking to realistic illustration to identify and sell a specific product.
- Although Waugh was free of many of the commercial restraints that impacted poster designers engaged by private companies, she still had to "sell" the parks. Yet, she retained considerable creative freedom: she was not usually obliged to depict an identifiable place or event, and Wirth clearly trusted her to invent a compelling new look for the NPS.

State Parks for Recreation, 1936

Dorothy Waugh (1896–1996)

Private Collection

- In the 1920s, despite their growth, the national parks could barely keep up with urbanites' demand for diversion. After a long and costly journey—the parks were still remote for most Americans—visitors would frequently arrive to find a park overrun by other tourists. Yet, it was far from easy to create new national parks: the law required that any site be unique, representing "the highest type of its particular features [with] duplication to be avoided."
- On the other hand, parks established by the *states* were not subject to such lofty standards. Roosevelt, keen to stimulate local economies, responded enthusiastically to the popular clamor for more state parks at sites of local or regional significance.
- In a Fauvist palette bursting with vibrant contrasting colors, Waugh's fragmented yet peaceful composition features two horseback riders crossing a lush plain. The text in the lower register inventories the season's varied recreational opportunities.

State Parks FOR RECREATION
Dorothy Waugh
hiking fishing riding picnicking
boating swimming camping skiing

STATE PARKS
Dorothy Waugh

State Parks [Grilling], 1936

Dorothy Waugh (1896–1996)

Private Collection

- Tasked with supervising the vast expansion of the state park system, Conrad Wirth implemented a win-win approach: if a state supplied the land, the CCC would provide free labor to develop it. In support of the program, Waugh's State Parks poster series emphasizes these parks as a whole, along with the scenic and recreational opportunities now within geographic reach of virtually all Americans.
- Campfire cooking in the national parks was common from the outset, and in the larger parks it became a feature of package trips arranged by the lodges. By the 1920s, visitors using the parks' free automobile camps often brought along their own camp stoves. By the mid-1930s, outdoor grilling had become a quintessential part of American culture, and grills and picnic pavilions constructed by the CCC were ubiquitous.
- Waugh's succinct poster reinforces the public's association of this beloved activity with the NPS in just two words: "State Parks." The family stands in the snow but radiates contentment amid the warmest of palettes.

State Parks [Year-Round Recreation], 1936

Dorothy Waugh (1896–1996)

Private Collection

- Between 1933 and 1942, 771 state parks were built or enlarged in almost every state—an explosive level of growth that advanced the state-park movement by some fifty years and changed the recreational habits of the nation.
- Public recreation in the state parks met so many of the Roosevelt administration's aspirations: it was accessible, it was affordable (admission was generally free), and it generated health, social, and economic benefits through wholesome activities in nature.
- With seven figures organized into warm- and cold-weather sections, Waugh's poster, like its counterparts, highlights year-round recreation. The composition presents a montage of activities, and because the figures are what matter most, scenic elements are restricted to tiny balls.

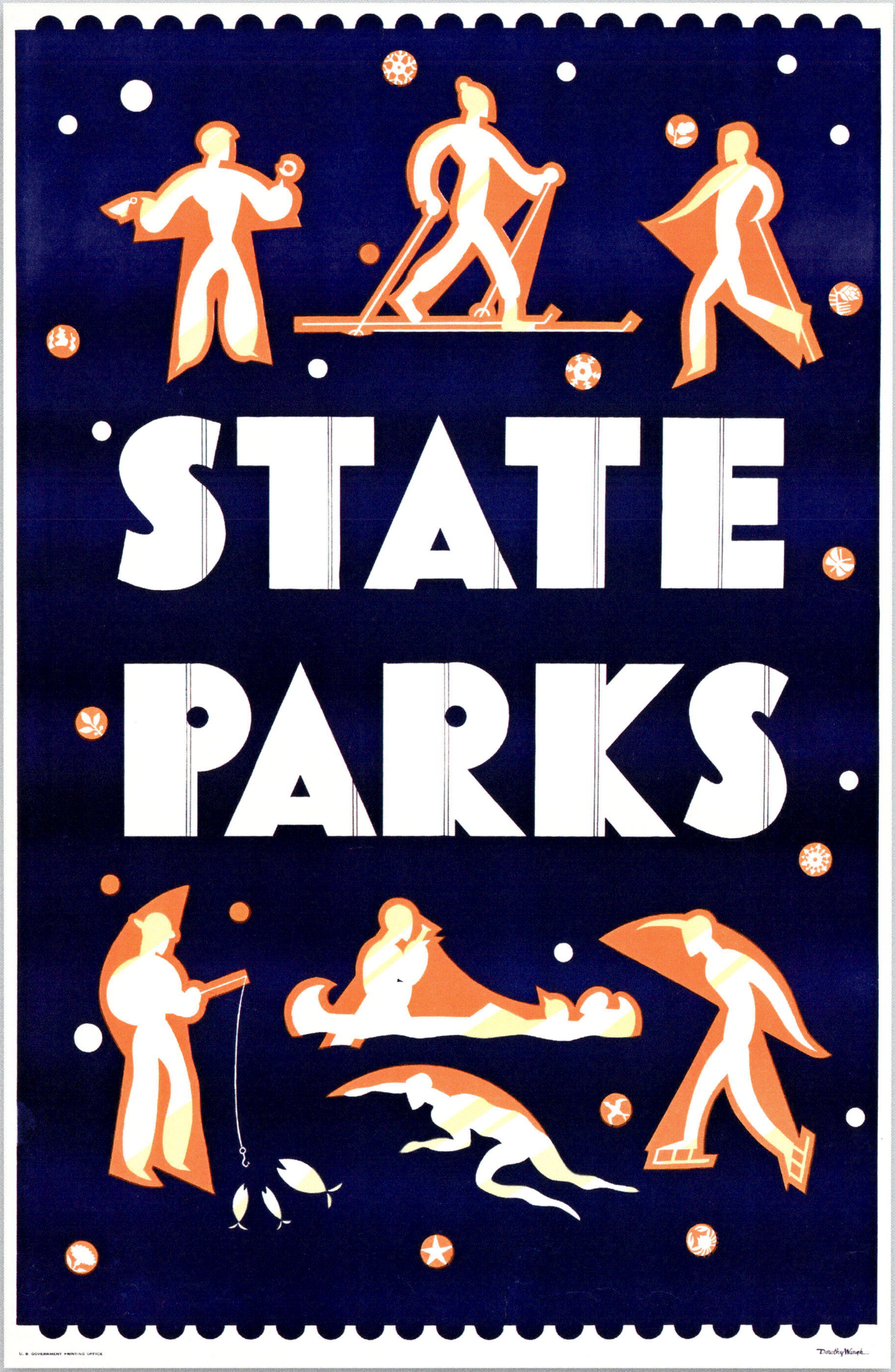
STATE
PARKS
U. S. GOVERNMENT PRINTING OFFICE
Dorothy Waugh

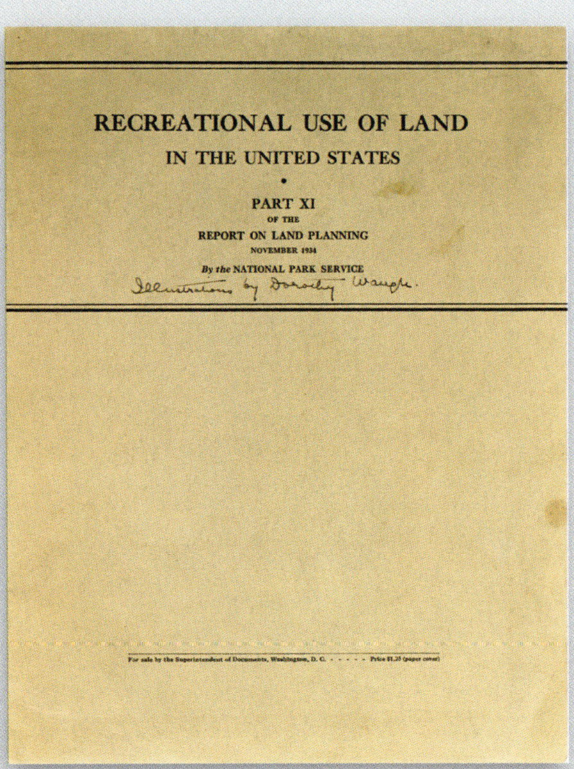

RECREATIONAL USE OF LAND
IN THE UNITED STATES
•
PART XI
OF THE
REPORT ON LAND PLANNING
NOVEMBER 1934
By the NATIONAL PARK SERVICE
Illustrations by Dorothy Waugh.

For sale by the Superintendent of Documents, Washington, D. C. - - - - - Price $1.25 (paper cover)

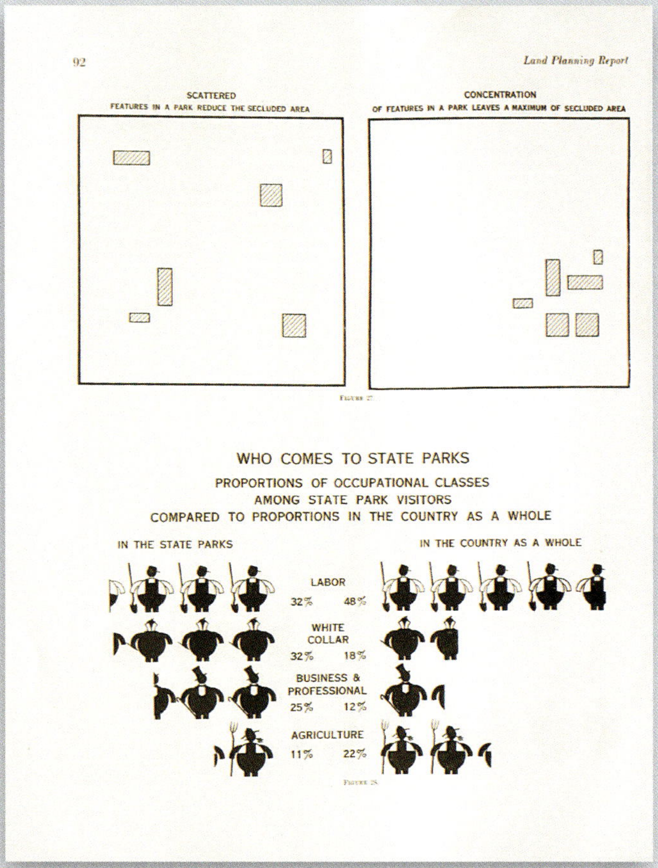

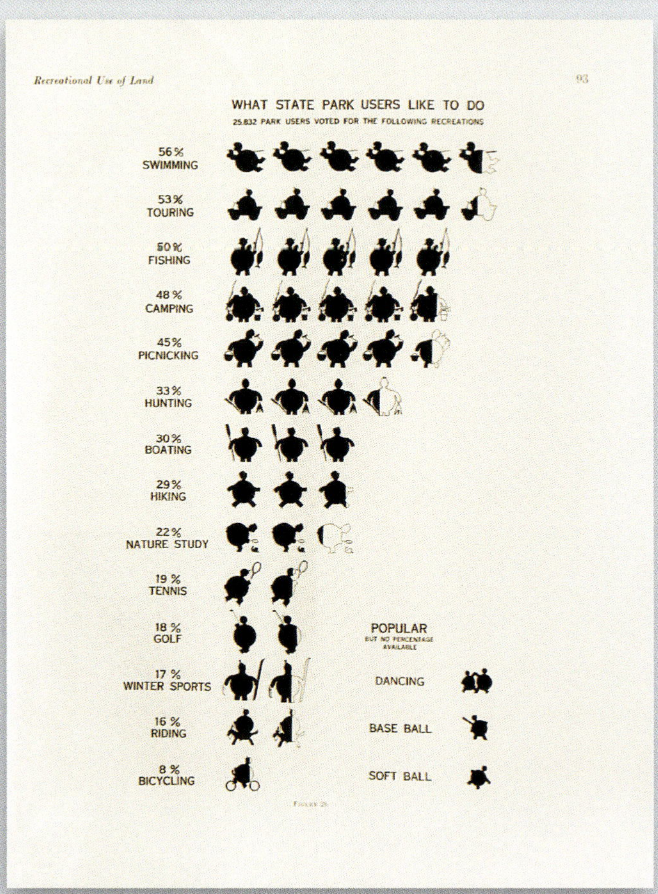

Recreational Use of Land in the United States, 1934

Illustration and Production: Dorothy Waugh (1896–1996)

Left: *Courtesy of The Jones Library, Inc., Amherst, Massachusetts*

Right: *Courtesy of National Park Service, National Park Service History Collection, HFCA 29996*

- This massive NPS report, commissioned by the Roosevelt administration, was key in the government's implementation of the most extensive recreation program in the nation's history. Waugh oversaw the report's production.
- Because of the report's density, Wirth also enlisted Waugh to create accompanying images and diagrams that would distill data, illustrate the report's "story," and even inject some humor. Waugh's contributions, advanced for the era, would today be called "infographics."
- The administration's preoccupation with recreation in nature derived partly from its concern about how unemployed city dwellers were using their time. The New Dealers asserted that "commercialized" diversions and "lying about" decreased productivity, undermined health and community, and increased crime and even subversiveness. Time spent in nature, on the other hand, might diminish the undesirable effects of "unnatural" urban environments.

Historic National Parks and Monuments, 1935

Dorothy Waugh (1896–1996)

Private Collection

- During the Depression, there was great popular interest in all things American. Many looked to the country's history, often critically, in an effort to make sense of the wrenching and divisive crisis. The Roosevelt administration, however, sought to affirm positive aspects of the American experience. New Dealers believed that a cultural understanding based on Americans' shared history and traditions could unite the nation around a "usable past"—and contribute to a better future. They asserted that knowledge of the country's history was a mark of good citizenship.
- The national parks and monuments contributed greatly to the government's effort. The monuments are sites designated, by a president, as important in archaeological, natural, and national history. Although their oversight had been spread among several agencies, in 1933 the Roosevelt administration consolidated it under the NPS, resulting in fifty-seven new areas for the bureau to manage—an immediate threefold increase.
- The posters Waugh created for this series are her first to depict specific locations and people. This Art Deco poster, intended to promote many monuments simultaneously, serves as both a travel poster and a historical document. Secretary of the Interior Harold Ickes reportedly loathed the design, but it had already been distributed.
- The seven floating commemorative busts represent a Puebloan, Captain John Smith, George Washington, a frontiersman, Abraham Lincoln, Robert E. Lee, and a Union soldier. The locations associated with them are simply written down on white stripes—unsurprising, as many of these places were by that time overgrown fields that offered little of visual interest. The meandering stripes also comprise a kind of tourist road map; and in the context of the poster's red, white, and blue palette, they evoke a waving American flag.

HISTORIC
MOUND CITY
JAMESTOWN
MESA VERDE
CHACO CANYON
FORT MATANZAS
FORT MARION
LEE MANSION
BIRTHPLACE
GETTYSBURG
COWPENS
CASTLE PINCKNEY
CHANCELLORSVILLE
STONES RIVER
CHATTANOOGA
MISSIONARY RIDGE
ANTIETAM
FORT DONELSON
CHICKAMAUGA
SHILOH
APPOMATTOX
DOROTHY WAUGH
NATIONAL PARKS
AND MONUMENTS
U. S. GOVERNMENT PRINTING OFFICE

PUEBLOS OF THE SOUTHWEST
DOROTHY WAUGH
National Parks
& Monuments
U. S. GOVERNMENT PRINTING OFFICE

> "Americans have always looked to history
> for a sense of national cohesiveness,
> especially in times of crisis,
> when cohesiveness is under siege."
>
> **—Peter Conn, historian**

National Parks and Monuments/Pueblos of the Southwest,

1935

Dorothy Waugh (1896–1996)

Private Collection

- The NPS's expanded oversight of the nation's monuments provided an opportunity to enhance the bureau's profile, increase the number of visitors to these notable and underpublicized sites, and encourage support for historic preservation.
- In 1906, President Theodore "Teddy" Roosevelt (Franklin D. Roosevelt's distant cousin) had established Mesa Verde National Park in Colorado as the first park to "preserve the works of man." Abandoned for centuries before the park's founding, the area features magnificent structures made by the Ancestral Puebloans between 550 and 1300 AD, including stone dwellings several stories high and built into the sheltering alcoves of the canyon wall. Today, the park is a UNESCO World Heritage Site.
- By the time Waugh produced this poster, there were several other national parks and monuments once occupied by Ancestral Puebloans; her design promotes them all. She further enlivens the compelling subject with an earthy southwestern palette, distinctive lettering, and a purple sky.

WILDLIFE PROTECTION: THE SERIES THAT WASN'T

Save Our Wildlife [Trumpeter Swan], 1935

Dorothy Waugh (1896–1996)

Private Collection

- The Dust Bowl disasters encouraged the development of ecological and wildlife management systems, with the federal government establishing or reinforcing agencies and staffing them with scientists.
- In 1935, for a joint campaign by the National Park Service and the Department of Agriculture's Biological Survey, Waugh was to design posters featuring five emblematic endangered animals—starting with a trumpeter swan, whose preservation had motivated the Survey to create a wildlife refuge near Yellowstone. Characteristically, Waugh's dramatic poster of the swan, which was well received, combined realistic and abstract elements.
- NPS scientists called Waugh's proposal sketch for the next poster, of a bighorn sheep, "well-nigh perfect." At substantial expense, the bureau printed 5,000 copies of the sheep poster to ensure its broad distribution to conservationists, park officials, nature and game clubs, and schools. The Survey, however, deemed the poster insufficiently realistic and disliked the style of its lettering. With great reluctance, the NPS destroyed all 5,000 copies.
- The remainder of the series was abandoned, as the NPS recognized that it would not make headway with a partner who now considered Waugh's modernism ill-suited to the purpose.

TRUMPETER SWAN
SAVE OUR
WILD LIFE
DEPARTMENT OF THE INTERIOR
NATIONAL PARK SERVICE
BIOLOGICAL SURVEY
DEPARTMENT OF AGRICULTURE
DOROTHY WAUGH
U. S. GOVERNMENT PRINTING OFFICE

Original illustration for *Warm Earth*, 1943

Dorothy Waugh (1896–1996)

Courtesy of The Jones Library, Inc., Amherst, Massachusetts

- Although the *Save Our Wildlife* series was canceled because of its modernist depiction, Waugh had, in fact, frequently been touted as a "master of realistic scientific illustration."
- Waugh's book *Warm Earth* is one of many examples of that talent. The text and illustrations highlight aspects of the natural world, from soil formation to the growth of plants. *The New York Times* declared that Waugh's compositions were "drawn with the beauty that the artist's eye sees . . . and accuracy that comes from careful observation."

Poster Stickers, 1936

Dorothy Waugh (1896–1996)

Private Collection

- In 1936, Waugh designed fifty small "poster stickers" for the NPS. Because the stickers generally depicted specific locations and subjects, their style was more realistic than the full-size posters of the campaign. Printed in very large runs, they were intended as free souvenirs for those who visited the parks or requested them from the government. An untold number of Americans affixed them to letters, packages, and the like. The director of the NPS praised the stickers as offering a new way to "spread the gospel of the parks."
- The stickers represented all of the national parks as well as some national monuments and state parks, and they referred to recreation, history, and wildlife.
- Perhaps reflecting the ambivalence about automobiles in the parks, one sticker shows just a glimpse of a tire. Although increased park access by car improved visitor numbers, preservationists considered the automobile (and accompanying roads and park development) a curse.

RECREATION in your NATIONAL PARKS
MAMMOTH CAVE NATIONAL PARK
RECREATION in your NATIONAL PARKS
NATIONAL PARK
RECREATION in your National Parks
Acadia NATIONAL PARK
HISTORY in your National Parks
State Parks
HISTORY in your National Parks
STATE PARKS
Yosemite NATIONAL PARK
STATE PARKS
RECREATION in your NATIONAL PARKS
STATE PARKS
winter sports NATIONAL PARKS
RECREATION in your STATE PARKS
Wild Flowers in your NATIONAL PARKS
State Parks
Zion NATIONAL PARK
STATE PARKS
NATIONAL PARKS
State Parks
Grand Canyon NATIONAL PARK
BOATING in your STATE PARKS
HAWAII NATIONAL PARK
STATE PARKS
SHENANDOAH NATIONAL PARK
HISTORY in your STATE PARKS
Platt National Park
STATE PARKS
Rocky Mountain NATIONAL PARK
HIKING in your STATE PARKS
Glacier NATIONAL PARK
State Parks
Yellowstone NATIONAL PARK
WILDLIFE in your NATIONAL PARKS
Carlsbad Caverns National Park
STATE PARKS
Mt. Rainier NATIONAL PARK
DEATH VALLEY NATIONAL MONUMENT for Winter Vacations
MT. McKINLEY NATIONAL PARK
Wind Cave NATIONAL PARK
Custer STATE PARK
the Badlands
SOUTH DAKOTA
GRAND TETON NATIONAL PARK
Mt. Olympus NATIONAL MONUMENT
BRYCE CANYON NATIONAL PARK
the Colorful Southwest
PETRIFIED FORESTS
NATURAL BRIDGES
CLIFF DWELLINGS
EARLY MISSIONS
INDIANS OF TODAY
in your National Monuments
Hot Springs NATIONAL PARK
Lassen Volcanic NATIONAL PARK
Mesa Verde NATIONAL PARK

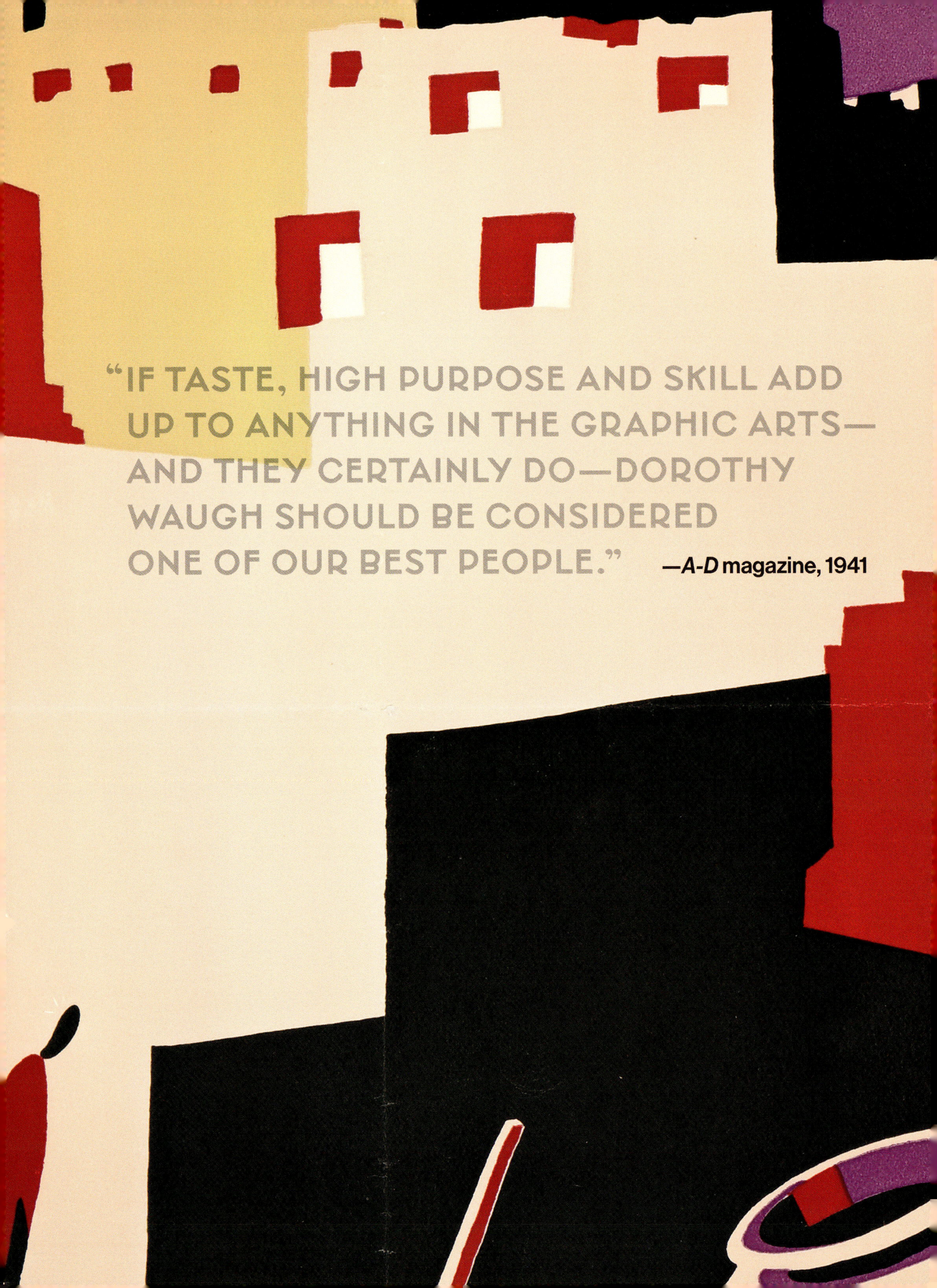

"IF TASTE, HIGH PURPOSE AND SKILL ADD UP TO ANYTHING IN THE GRAPHIC ARTS—AND THEY CERTAINLY DO—DOROTHY WAUGH SHOULD BE CONSIDERED ONE OF OUR BEST PEOPLE." —*A-D* magazine, 1941

A LEGACY OF GOVERNMENT POSTERS

In 1937, Waugh left the National Park Service to head Alfred A. Knopf's Books for Young People in New York City. Although she never returned to poster design, Waugh's NPS campaign set the stage for the subsequent deluge of government-issued posters. Many other agencies, including the Federal Art Project, the Rural Electrification Administration, and multiple World War II propaganda bureaus soon mounted highly ambitious campaigns of their own.

Aided by the rapid growth of the graphic design profession, the surge in government posters would continue through much of the twentieth century. Officials used the succinct and visually powerful medium to convey an expanding range of messages that differed vastly from those of private enterprise. Posters addressed public health, the Cold War, the space program, social concerns, and national security. Their proliferation was also a matter of necessity, helping to secure the public's attention amid ubiquitous private-sector advertising.

TIMBERLINE LODGE
MOUNT HOOD NATIONAL FOREST
O R E G O N
A MILE HIGH WINTER PLAYGROUND
FOR EVERYBODY

Timberline Lodge/Mount Hood National Forest, c. 1939

Kenneth Whitley (1918–79)

Poster House Permanent Collection

- By August 1935, when President Roosevelt established the Federal Art Project (FAP), Waugh had already completed the designs for most of the NPS posters. Although FAP officials consulted with her early in the program's formation (details of the meeting are unknown), historians have stated incorrectly that she was an FAP artist. Also inaccurate are claims that she worked in the FAP's preferred medium of silkscreen.
- The FAP ultimately produced some 30,000 designs, usually promoting a single event or topical subject for a government or civic client; only 2,000 of these have survived. This poster for the US Forest Service, clearly influenced by Waugh's work, highlights the government venture Timberline Lodge in Oregon, built and operated by the Works Progress Administration (WPA) on Forest Service land.
- The lodge opened in 1938 and began operating its Magic Mile Chairlift, then the world's longest, in 1939. Passenger chairlifts had originated in 1936 at Idaho's Sun Valley Resort; they were a milestone in the popularization of downhill skiing and quickly supplanted rope tows.

Rural Electrification Administration/Wash Day, 1937

Lester Beall (1903–69)

Private Collection

- Another federal agency would soon follow the NPS's lead, producing an extended poster campaign to advance its agenda. In 1937, the Rural Electrification Administration (REA), tasked with bringing affordable electricity to rural America, hired Lester Beall to design a campaign highlighting the advantages of electrification. When Beall began work on his three series of REA posters, he was not a very well-known graphic designer; four years and eighteen celebrated posters later, he was renowned in the US and abroad.
- Here, an electric washing machine, a device almost unheard of in 1930s rural America, dominates the interior of a silhouetted farmhouse, underscoring that laundry can now be done *inside* the home with the hot and cold running water that electricity provides.
- Although Waugh had worked as a full-time employee in continuous contact with NPS authorities, Beall and many subsequent designers worked for the government at arm's length, maintaining private practices that served other clients.

BEALL
WASH DAY
RURAL ELECTRIFICATION ADMINISTRATION

America's answer!
PRODUCTION
JEAN CARLU
U.S. GOVERNMENT PRINTING OFFICE
DIVISION OF INFORMATION
OFFICE FOR EMERGENCY MANAGEMENT

Production/America's Answer!, 1941

Jean Carlu (1900–97)

Private Collection

- By the time the United States entered World War II in December 1941, posters were crucial in widespread government messaging, and during the war, the US produced more posters than any other combatant. Some estimates of the number of individual designs reach 200,000—a questionable figure, but the actual number is undoubtedly extremely high.
- In May 1940, as America's anxiety about the war in Europe mounted, Roosevelt hurriedly established the Office for Emergency Management (OEM). The OEM hired Charles Coiner, the highly regarded art director of the N.W. Ayer and Son advertising agency, as its art consultant. During the agency's brief lifespan, Coiner enlisted leading designers to create modernist propaganda posters such as this one by French émigré Jean Carlu.
- Until the US entered the war, "America's answer" was to support the Allies by producing munitions and other military supplies. Here, Carlu executes Coiner's preliminary design concept: a disembodied gloved hand grips a wrench—a weapon of production—in an image signifying the nation's impending release of its mighty power.
- In June 1942, six months after his declaration of war, Roosevelt replaced the OEM with the Office of War Information (OWI). OWI launched a huge, multimedia propaganda effort, in which posters continued to play a prominent role but now relied on realistic or literal depictions to convey their messages. Modernist compositions had fallen decisively from favor, succumbing to the same aesthetic objections Waugh experienced with the aborted Wildlife series.

Grand Canyon National Park, 1938

Designer Unknown

Grand Canyon National Park Museum Collection, GRCA 122699

National Parks USA, 1968

Ansel Adams (1902–84)

Poster House Permanent Collection

- In the decades following Waugh's campaign, the NPS commissioned many other striking posters, works that continued Waugh's legacy even as they employed different styles and printing methods. Two compelling examples are shown here.
- Between 1938 and 1941, WPA and CCC artists working at the National Park Service's Western Museum Laboratories (WML) in Berkeley, California, designed at least fifteen silkscreened posters promoting the parks, including this one for the Grand Canyon. Stylized, but still more realistic than Waugh's posters, they promoted the ranger naturalist service and other programs for visitors. Very few copies from this series have survived; two are known only from photographs and one only from a WML monthly report.
- In 1968, a series of six designs by Ansel Adams ushered in a new heyday for NPS posters, which would last through the mid-1980s. Like the other five in the series, this design, promoting the Canyon de Chelly, features Adams's renowned black-and-white photography. His image contrasts starkly with the colorful geometries of Waugh's depiction of the same Ancestral Puebloan structures.

A FREE GOVERNMENT SERVICE
GRAND CANYON
NATIONAL PARK
U.S. DEPARTMENT OF THE INTERIOR
NATIONAL PARK SERVICE

national parks usa

Boston
a new national park...
Boston National Historical Park:
Faneuil Hall
Paul Revere House
Old North Church
Old South Meeting House
Old State House
Bunker Hill
Charlestown Navy Yard
National Park Service
U.S. Department of the Interior

Liberté
Liberty
A gift of the French people,
this colossal statue at the portal to the New World embodies
man's ceaseless quest for freedom and dignity.
In its century of vigil, it has greeted millions
of the oppressed and the venturous
and is known around the world as the very symbol of America.
Statue of Liberty National Monument
New York
National Park Service
U.S. Department of the Interior

Boston, a new national park, 1975

Paul Rand (1914–96)

Private Collection

Liberté Liberty, 1986

Massimo Vignelli (1931–2014)

Massimo and Lella Vignelli papers, Vignelli Center for Design Studies, Rochester Institute of Technology

- Designated a national park in late 1974, Boston National Historical Park is a collection of landmarks that showcase the city's role in the American Revolution. This poster by Paul Rand, a towering figure of mid-twentieth-century graphic design, celebrates the new park in a characteristically simple and playful design—the result, in fact, of his renowned creative discipline. Characteristic, too, is Rand's use of symbols open to multiple interpretations: the starlike form is also a stick figure holding a light that, amid a thoroughly patriotic composition, recalls both Paul Revere and his midnight ride and Lady Liberty.
- Massimo Vignelli's 1986 poster of the Statue of Liberty National Monument uses many of the design elements of the Unigrid—a system he designed for use across virtually all NPS publications when he created the bureau's new visual identity in 1977. In order to increase design efficiency and decrease costs, the Unigrid, still in use today, standardizes formatting and production with an array of consistent graphic components and an unseen grid layout. In this poster, Vignelli joins the Waugh lineage, but in his uniquely systematic way.

COLOPHON

Editor

Alexandra Hoff

Copy Editor

Anne Cook

Design and Production

Marnie Soom

Typefaces

Tablet Gothic

Broadacre